Quick Help For MacOS

Catalina Users

MacOS Catalina for seniors: learn how to use mac catalina from setup to features & troubleshooting

Ryan C. Bernard

Quick Help

For

MacOS Catalina

Users

MacOS Catalina for seniors: learn how to use mac catalina from setup to features & troubleshooting

Ryan C. Bernard

Dedicated to all my readers

Contents

Introduction

It was only late 2019 that the new macOS; macOS Catalina came out and of course, you're looking for how to install it on your Macs. If you have a Mac that's compatible, you can install this on your computer safely. Just as you get with older versions of the macOS, the new Catalina comes with different cool updates and upgrades.

It's free to install and the process is straightforward depending on the method you choose to use. Even when following the safe route, there are still certain problems you could face on the way. So in this guide, we'll be talking about how you can install the new macOS Catalina on your Mac.

You'll want to first check if your Mac is compatible with Catalina. It might be tempting to upgrade to the new OS but you should take the time to see if this suits your system. If you have a MacBook from 2012 and later, you should be able to install Catalina on your machine.

If you don't really know how old your Mac is, you can go to the **About This Mac** section of your computer to check. Another way to gauge if your Mac makes it is if it could run macOS 10.14 Mojave. If it could run that then it should work with Catalina.

1

MacOS Catalina Setup

Should I do a clean install or standard installation?

When you want to update your computer to run the latest software like Catalina, you have a decision to make; will you set things up from scratch like you just got a new Mac or will you just do a simple upgrade while still keeping your settings.

These options have their pros and cons and it all comes down to personal choice.

With a **Clean Install**, you get everything new. You can choose how you would like to arrange new settings. You aren't confined to the former settings of the older macOS version. Doing a clean install allows you to remove any bloat on the Mac.

This also gets rid of your downloads and apps so that your Mac is truly fresh and clean. You can easily back up to cloud services like iCloud or Dropbox so that you can still access the files that have been backed up.

You can still download the apps that were on your Mac from the App Store. One awesome perk to this is that you can truly examine if you need to re-download certain apps that were on your Mac before the clean install. If there's an app you found you really didn't use that much, you wouldn't have to waste your time installing it on the 'new Mac'

The downside to doing a clean install is that you need to have patience. This method takes more time to get up and running. Apart from the stress required for a clean install, you'll also need to do things like signing in to iCloud again, entering passwords for apps like Mail, getting your pictures from the cloud and other little things that make the process take forever.

The clean install process is tricky and a little complex for srrrrrrrrrrrrrrrrrrrrrrome but if you have the patience and the time to do a clean install, then this may just be the way to go for you.

Unlike a clean install where all your settings and adjustments are gone, the **Standard Installation** keeps your stuff. When you install a new macOS with the standard install method, your files, apps, documents and settings will be exactly where you left them before you made the upgrade.

You save yourself the stress of going to iCloud to get back your pictures and also signing into different apps. As a result, this process is so much faster and straightforward.

It's just like repainting the walls in your house to purple. You would still recognize your bedroom, you would still know where the kitchen or the bathroom is at but they'll only be in a different color. Unlike a clean install where you are moving to an entirely new house already painted purple but you now have to start arranging your furniture, hanging picture frames and getting used to where the rooms are at.

If you don't want the stress of downloading apps over again and doing and the process necessary for a clean install, then just do the basic standard installation and you'll be good to go.

How to set up macOS Catalina using standard installation

Installing macOS Catalina is hard enough for some people so if anything, they'll need a process that will make it easier. And it doesn't get simpler than installing with the standard install process. These are the steps to upgrading to the latest macOS on your computer

1. As we mentioned at the outset, you want to check if your Mac is compatible with Catalina. you can head over to the Apple page to see if your Mac

makes   the   cut

https://support.apple.com/HT210222

2. The next thing you want to do is back up your computer. When you want to do major things like move to a new OS, the worst thing you can do is not back up your files. It's so easy for things to wrong and without a backup, your files and documents are toast. If you don't know how to back up your Mac, there's a guide on that below.

3. The next thing you'll want to do is to download macOS Catalina. You can easily get it from the App Store

- Hit the **A** icon on the dock to launch the **App Store**
- Press the search bar along the upper left of the screen
- Enter **macOS Catalina** in the search field and search
- When you see Catalina, select it to open the details screen

4. Hit the blue **Get** button to download the Catalina installer on your computer. This could take quite some time, after all, it is 8.16GB. Simply exercise patience and it should open when it downloads.

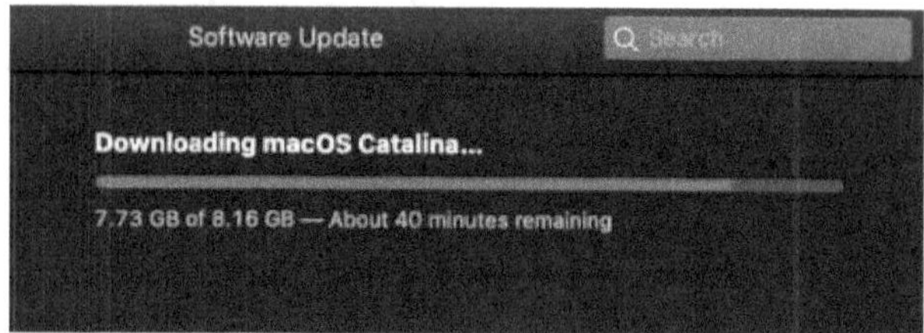

- It is vital that you have a full battery when doing this so be sure to connect the computer to power. One of the worst things that can happen is the Mac shutting down in the middle of installation, it just spells 'severe data loss'

5. Once it's loaded, go through with the instructions to start installing the new OS on your computer. You can choose to install it to another partition if you want. Your computer could restart a couple of times while it's installing. When the installation is finished, you will be taken to the login page for macOS Catalina.

How to set up macOS Catalina using custom install

If you don't want to upgrade to Catalina using the standard installation method, you can do the clean install method and use the bootable USB Drive. Using the standard installations allows you to keep your data and apps but with a bootable UB drive, you can install the new macOS Catalina on different Macbooks.

If you notice that your computer is behaving strangely, a clean install might just be the way out to stopping that and making it work normally again. Then again as you use your computer over the years, the disk space could have been occupied by some third-party and junk files, a clean install will help you get rid of that.

To start, you will want to dedicate about 2 hours to this and have a 16GB USB thumb drive (it should also be fresh). You'll also want to make sure that you use Time Machine to have a complete backup of your device so that if anything goes wrong, you can still restore the computer to how it was before you started dissecting

1. The next thing you'll want to do is to download macOS Catalina. You can easily get it from the App Store
   - Hit the **A** icon on the dock to launch the **App Store**
   - Press the search bar along the upper left of the screen
   - Enter **macOS Catalina** in the search field and search

- Select Catalina and hit **Get** to download it

2. After the download is finished, click the **Quit install macOS** button to quit the window for the installer

3. After that, bring up the Terminal. If you don't know how to get to this,

   - Enter the **Applications** section

   - Choose **Utilities**

   - Then select **Terminal**

4. In the Terminal window, enter the word **sudo** and hit space

5. Launch a Finder window and move to the folder for **Application**. When you find the macOS 10.15 installer file, right click on it. From the dropdown menu, choose **Show Package Contents**

6. Within the installer file, move to the **Contents** then **Resources**

7. Find the file titled **createinstallmedia.** When you see it, click and drag it to the Terminal window

8. Now, you'll want to type this in the Terminal window **/Applications/Install\ macOS\ Catalina.app/Contents/Resources/createinstallmedia –volume /Volumes/XXXX**

Do you notice the XXXX at the end? Don't type that, you'll want to substitute that with the USB drive's name that you would like to use

9. After adding the name of the USB drive, run the command. When asked, add your admin password

10. When asked, enter **Y** and hit Enter. What will happen is that the Catalina installer will be created on the USB drive. It won't be completed instantly so you'll have to allow it to run and when it's done, you should see the "Install media now available" message

   - You may be asked if you would like to install Xcode. Simply choose the **Not now** option to complete the process safely

When the bootable Catalina installer has been created on the USB drive, continue by rebooting the Mac and when you hear the reboot sound, press and hold the **Option** button.

11. Select the option for **Install macOS Catalina**. You can use the arrow keys on the keyboard or the mouse pointer to navigate.

12. From the **Utilities** window, choose **Disk Utility** when the drive has been booted. From the list on the screen select the startup drive for your Mac and press **Erase**

13. Go back to the **Utilities** window after the startup disk has been formatted, and choose **Install macOS**. When you are prompted to choose where to install the operating system, select the startup drive you just erased and go through with the instructions to complete the process.

One reason why people use this process to install a new macOS is that they'll be able to install the operating system on another MacBook with the same installer. If you want to do this, just turn off the second Mac you want to install Catalina on and connect the USB installer to the computer. Turn on the Mac and hit the **Option** button when the reboot sound comes on. Go through with the steps above to continue to install Catalina on the Mac.

How to back up your Mac

The go-to tool for backing up a Mac is Time Machine. It's a wonderful way to make backups into an external drive. The best part of Time Machine is that it's not a third-party app you have to install from the App Store; it's baked into macOS so your Mac should have it already.

It's very easy to set up Time Machine on your Mac. These are the steps

1. Start by plugging your hard drive to your Mac.
   - If this is your first time connecting the hard drive to this computer, a pop-up might show up to confirm if you would like to use Time Machine. If you see this window, simply choose **Use As A Backup Disk** from the menu and you can skip all the following steps
2. If you don't see the pop-up, you'll have to enter the System Preferences. From the Apple menu at the upper left corner of the screen, choose the **System Preferences**

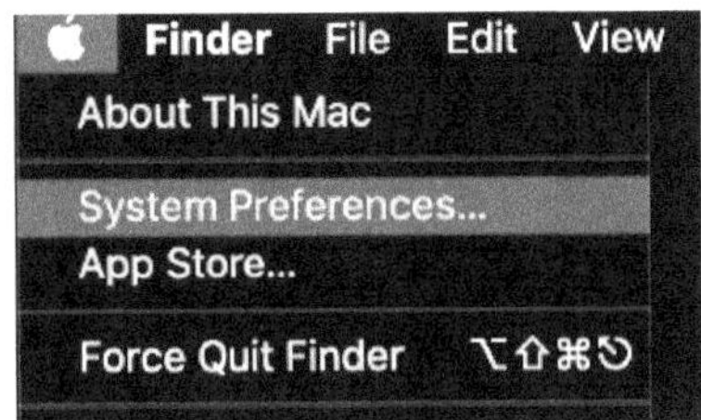

3. Select the icon for **Time Machine**

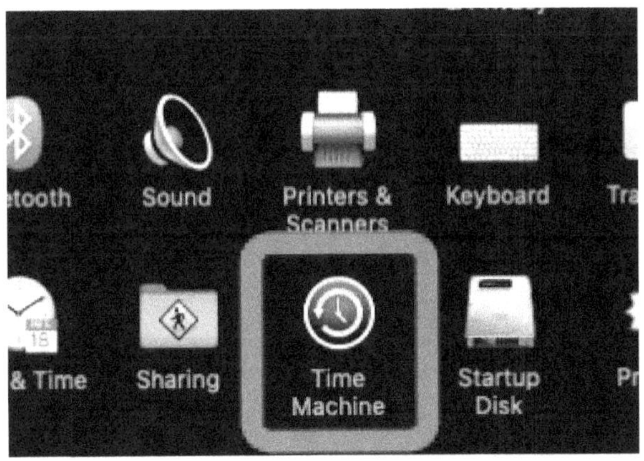

4. Choose **Select Backup Disk**

5. Pick the drive that you'll like to use as a backup for Time Machine

6. Tick the box for **Back Up Automatically** so that backups will be made automatically to the selected disks

2

MacOS Catalina Tips and Tricks

Doing conversions in Spotlight

With the Spotlight feature on your Mac, you can easily find files on your computer as well as preview them for quick access. It's a great and easy way to open applications and search for things on the web. But this function also serves as a calculator to calculate simple things.

You can also use this for basic conversions of any kind like if you want to convert a currency, length, mass and speed. You don't need any special command line to make this work, you just have to summon Spotlight by hitting **Cmd + Space**.

When Spotlight comes up, type in the number you want to convert with the value it is to be converted to, like "$37 in Euros". The best part of this is that you don't need to complete what you are typing before you get results. As you type in the currency "$37", you would already see the equivalent in different currencies.

You can only get common currencies from this preview like Euros, British Pounds, Canadian Dollars and others. But if you want to convert to a currency not listed there, just make sure to type in your request in full like "$37 in krone"

You can also type in symbols or labels to get other metrics. Like for example, if you simply type in 45 mm, you can convert it from millimeters to something else. When you hit **Enter** after typing in a calculation, it will be opened in the calculator.

Siri on your Mac

With the help of dictation, the MacBook's ability to listen when you speak got better when macOS Sierra came in 2016. But now, with Siri in macOS Catalina, the computer's ability to listen to speech has vastly improved.

You can summon Siri by hitting the Siri button in the menu bar or on the dock. You can also press and hold **Cmd + Space** to summon the assistant you use every day on your smartphone. If you have got a newer MacBook, you just call out the assistant by saying "Hey Siri". This way you can use the assistant hands-free.

While you can do the usual and ask Siri some questions like what the result of the game was or the situation of the weather, you can also use the assistant to turn off some functions on the computer like Bluetooth and Wi-Fi. If you are feeling lazy, you can just tell Siri to bring up certain files on the computer or to even open applications.

If you can use the Hey, Siri feature on your Mac, simply call

for the assistant and speak your request.

Taking screenshots on your Mac

The screenshot feature has been available on Windows for some time now. You can get a full shot of the screen by hitting the PrtSc button on the keyboard. If you just want a section of the screen, there's the good old Snipping Tool.

The hassle of this is that not all keyboards have that shortcut and you need to open up a separate app; Snipping Tool just to take a screenshot. Think of how you take screenshots on your iPhone. Do you have to go to the home screen and open the "**Screenshot**" app? No, you get it through shortcuts, the same way the Mac does it.

If you would like to take a screenshot on your Mac, just hit **Cmd + Shift + 3** simultaneously and you have your screenshot saved on the desktop. If you would like to capture just one section of the screen, simply hit **Cmd + Shift + 4**. If you would like to capture just one window, hit

Cmd + Shift + 4 press Space and then the window you want to get a shot of

For those with the latest MacBook Pro that has the infamous Touch Bar, you can hit **Cmd + Shift + 6** if you would like to capture the bar. With macOS Catalina, you get a preview of what you've captured on the lower part of the screen. To get a markup menu, you can click the preview and you can add notes to the screenshot. A quick and convenient way to take screenshots, plus a markup window? Yes, please.

Show and hide the menu bar

Ever since the Mac came out, the menu bar has been a regular feature. But more recently, you have the option to hide the menu bar. It's not that the menu bar is a nuisance or anything like that, but hiding it is definitely part of some personalization features you want to try on your system.

1. Enter the System Preferences section by selecting the Apple menu and choose **System Preferences**.
2. Click **General**
3. Choose the option for **Automatically hide and show the menu bar**

Checking the box will make the menu disappear but it isn't gone for good. Since you don't need this Apple menu on the screen every time, Apple created a system where the menu will only show when you slide or move to the upper part of the screen. Cool, right?

Use those unusual characters

Yes, you have the usual alphabets and numeric keys on your keyboard but you can also get more unusual characters from your Macs keyboard. Most people know that they add accents to letters in words like **café.** All you just do is press and hold the letter E and you will get more options. You can also hit Option + E for this. But you are not limited to his, there more of these exotic letters.

When you are in an app, enter the **Edit** menu. Most apps should have this along the top. At the bottom will be the Special Characters. From here, you get access to different symbols that you can use in your documents.

Of course, they'll be third party apps that don't support this which is normal. But for the apps where you get the option for this, it certainly is cool.

How to sign a document with Preview

With the Preview on your Mac, you can add notes, shapes as well as speech bubbles to your images easily. You can also create signatures and use them on a PDF or any photo you want. The signature feature is one of the most helpful tools provided.

Before this, you have no other option but to print out the document, use your good old pen to add your signature and then scan it back again. You may be thinking of using a fancy font but Preview provides a better way out.

1. Fire up **Preview**. You can also just click and drag a file to the Preview which you would find in the Dock. You can also double click an image or PDF and it will be launched in Preview automatically

2. Select the icon for Markup toolbox. It's the icon that looks like a pen in a circle and clicking it will show you the available tools for editing.

3. The editing bar will present the options for Text selection, then Sketch, Shapes and so on. You'll also find an indecipherable handwriting icon, select this, it's the Signature icon.

4. You should find any signature that has been created from this page. But if this is your first time using this, choose **Create Signature**

5. You can use a Camera to make your signature or the Trackpad. The quicker method is to simply scribble it on your trackpad. When you are done, press any key. If you want the signature to be more accurate, use a stylus if you have one or just simply use your fingertip.

6. Even though the trackpad provides the easiest way, using the Camera is the most accurate. In this case, you will simply write the signature on a piece of paper like you would normally. hold the white piece of paper to your computer's webcam and try to match it to the guideline

7. Once you have created the signature, you'll now want to add it to an image or PDF file

8. Start by opening the PDF or image you would like to add the signature to.

9. Navigate to the part of the document where you want the signature should be. There could be several pages on the document so it's better to be on the right one before you use the Signature tool

10. After you launch the toolbar, choose the Signature icon. You should find the signature you just added there. Simply select it and it will show up in the middle of your image. Move it to the right area.

Rename files in a batch

If you wanted to rename a group of files simultaneously, you'll have to enlist the help of a third-party software on your Mac. If you don't want that, you can use a rename script with AppleScript. But now with Catalina, the process is much easier.

You just have to select the files you would like to rename From the right-click menu, choose **Rename**. You can also select this in the Finder window
This will then show you the option to replace the text, add your own and basically do what you want.

Split Screen

One of the awesome things you can do with your MacBook is snap two different apps or windows to the opposite side of the screen. This is made possible as a result of the Split Screen feature.

Why would you even consider splitting your screen in the first place? It's basically for multitasking, rather than open one app after the other, you can have both of them on the screen so you can switch from one to the other easily. Especially now, when time is really of the essence, this feature is a lifesaver.

Previously, the way you can use this feature is by pressing and holding the **green maximize icon** in an app and then move it to the place you want it to be on the screen. But things have changed on the new macOS

On macOS Catalina, if you would like to use the split screen feature, you'll have to press and hold the same **green maximize icon** along the upper left hand part of the screen. This will then open a menu where you'll have the option to choose either Tile Window to Left of Screen, Tile Window to Right of Screen or to Enter Full Screen

You can also choose to move the window to a secondary screen if you have that. After you have opened a window on one side of the screen, you'll have to open a window or another app on the opposite side of the screen

When you open apps or windows in the Split Screen view, it will block the menu bar and launcher. This gives you more space to work with lesser icons. If you would like to work on 2 apps at once, using the split screen method is a good way to go

Using Windows on your Mac

If you are a long fan of the Mac, you probably won't be hungering to install Windows on your computer. But installing Windows does have its use like when you want to run some software or a cool game that's only available on Windows.

With Boot Camp Assistant, you can partition the hard drive to run Window on the hardware or you can use apps like VirtualBox to run Windows while still using your macOS.

Easy way to share with your friends

On the macOS, you can easily share files with your contacts and friends with the share button. It's basically the icon that looks like an arrow shooting out of a square. The nice thing about this is that your computer usually tracks who you share your files with frequently.

So if you regularly share files with Mike from work, the options to send it to him will be within arms reach. You should find the options along the lower part of the share section.

Use desktops on your Mac

With the help of Spaces, you can have several desktops on your computer. And these desktops come with their files and windows. If you would like to work on a project at a time without closing one, this feature will prove useful

On your trackpad, slide up with 4 fingers and hit the Mission Control option. To add a new desktop, hit the + button.

How to use Dark Mode

Since the bright light from the phone screens isn't particularly good for our eyes, different devices now have systems in place to help to combat it. It is said the blue light that comes from our devices can cause eyestrain and also prevent sleep.

On your Mac running macOS Catalina, you have the new Dark Mode feature that is set to come on at nighttime. With iOS 13, the Dark Mode feature also came to the phone and you'll also find it on your Apple TV. Before Dark Mode, you'll have to turn down the brightness of the screen to help with the eye straining issue.

The feature came in Mojave but with Catalina, you also have more options to use the feature. Before Dark Mode came in macOS Mojave, you could use the option for Night Shift. Apart from that, the only way you could get a dark theme is to darken the dock and the menu bar. You can find these in the System Preferences menu but if you are using Catalina, this is how you can enable it on your Mac

While you are setting up Catalina, you can opt to enable Dark Mode. If you did not set up Dark Mode at that time, you can still set it up later in the System Preferences settings

1. Hit the Apple menu along the top left corner of the screen and select **System Preferences**
2. Choose the option for **General**
3. From here, you can change different settings like the default browser. But we are here to change to Dark Mode so look in the **Appearance** section
4. Select the option for **Dark** with the dark interface to switch to Dark Mode on the Mac

When it nighttime and it feels like you need sunglasses to look at your computer screen, simply turn on Dark Mode. If you want to turn off Dark Mode, simply go through with the above steps but when you get to the Appearance section, select **Light** instead to revert back to the default theme.

Auto Dark Mode

The Dark Mode feature is nice and all but the issue with it is that it's not always ideal. Not many people like dealing with a dark display during the day, it makes it difficult to see what's on the screen. At the same time, they still want the cool dark theme that Dark Mode provides.

It would sure be nice if there's was a way to schedule Dark Mode so that it goes off at sunrise by itself and turn back on when it's getting dark. About a year ago, it would have been near impossible but macOS Catalina brings a new feature to the Mac; Auto Dark Mode.

The Auto Dark Mode option adjusts the screen from Dark to Light and vice versa automatically. You probably have a lot of things to do on your Mac and you certainly don't want to add toggling off and on Dark Mode to the list. If you would like to use the Auto Dark Mode feature on your Mac,

1. Hit the Apple menu along the top left corner of the screen and select **System Preferences**

2. Choose the option for **General**

3. In the **Appearance** section, you'll find the option for **Dark** which makes the interface darker and also **Light** for the default white template. But you'll also find **Auto** as the last option. Select this.

4. Right away, you'll see the theme adjust to the time of day. But you can still fine tune the time when Dark Mode kicks in with Night Shift. In the System Preferences menu, select **Displays**

5. Choose **Night Shift**

6. To set a custom schedule, choose **Custom**

Activity Viewer

With the Activity Viewer, you can now close different processes easily. All you do is select the processes you would like to quit and hit the close button.

The button was present before but it would become dormant when you select multiple processes. But now, the button remains active which provides a quicker way to terminate processes.

Block senders

These days, it's all too common to find companies sending you emails that you don't want. If someone or a business keeps sending you these frustrating emails, there's a better to stop them. The common method most people follow is selecting all the emails from the sender and deleting them.

Well, guess what? They'll keep sending more. MacOS makes it super easy to block senders with the built in Mail app. You just set up a filter in the app so that it deletes all of the emails from the sender. It's a quicker way to get rid of all messages from a sender but the best part is that it also blocks them from sending you stuff

To block senders in Mail,
1. Move to **Mail**
2. From the options that show up on the menu bar, select **Preferences**

3. To avoid entering the email address later on, you can just open up an email from the person and click **Mail** then **Preferences**

4. Along the top of the window, select **Rules** then **Add Rule**

5. If you opened an email from the sender before starting the process, you'll already find their email filled in. If you don't find their email, select the empty field beside **contains** and add the email address

6. If you would like to block emails from a domain and not just from one email address (that is all emails from @exampleemail.com and not just jenny@exampleemail.com) add only exampleemail.com in the empty field

7. Under that, you'll find the section for **Perform the following actions**. Choose **Delete Message** from the options that show up

8. In the empty field for description, add a description for the rule. You can type in something like **Blocked**

9. Select the **OK** button at the lower part of the screen

There's another way to block senders with the Mail app

1. Fire up the **Mail** app on your computer

2. Open up a message from the contact you want to block

3. Just above the message, you'll find the name of the sender. When you hover on it, select the arrow icon

4. Choose the option for **Block Contact**

Just like that, the messages will be driven out from your inbox. You can still change your mind and lift the ban. To do this, follow the same steps but choose **Unblock Contact** instead.

Hide windows fast

Maybe you want to conceal something from prying eyes or you just want more speed while working, pressing **Cmd + H** will hide a window very quickly. It doesn't close the app but it will go into the background so that you can access it again from the dock section

Use Screen Time on the Mac

MacOS Catalina brought many new features to the Mac and among them is the Screen Time feature. The main purpose of Screen Time is to help users measure how much they use their computers. With the help of limits that they set for themselves, users can see their usage stats.

If you have a child and you would like to place some restrictions, this feature works great as parental controls. With Screen Time, you can set how long your kids spend on certain websites and applications. If you would like to enable Screen Time on your computer

1. Enter the System Preferences settings by selecting the Apple menu at the top of the screen and selecting **System Preferences**

2. Among the different options shown, select **Screen Time**

3. In the panel along the left side of the screen, select **Options** at the very bottom

4. At upper right hand corner of the window, select **Turn On** to enable Screen Time on the computer

5. If you would like to disable the feature, follow the same steps listed above but when you select the **Options** button you'll find **Turn Off** instead. Click that to disable Screen Time

One thing you want to make sure that you do is set a password for Screen Time. The benefit of setting a Screen Time password is that you'll be able to secure your settings. With the password, you can also extend the time slot for others.

- Enter the System Preferences settings by selecting the Apple menu at the top of the screen and selecting **System Preferences**

- Among the different options shown, select **Screen Time**

- In the panel along the left side of the screen, select **Options** at the very bottom

- Just beside the option for **Use Screen Time Passcode**, tick the box. You'll be prompted to add the passcode for Screen Time

App limits on macOS Catalina

Another feature Catalina makes possible is setting limits for different applications. This also works for other websites as well. If you would like to set up app limits on your Mac, you would need to enable Screen Time.

After turning on Screen Time, follow these steps to add an app limit

1. Enter the System Preferences settings by selecting the Apple menu at the top of the screen and selecting **System Preferences**
2. Among the different options shown, select **Screen Time**
3. In the panel along the left side of the screen, select **App Limits**
4. At the upper right hand corner of the window, select **Turn On** to enable App Limits

5. After turning on App Limits, hit the **+** icon along the bottom. This will allow you to choose app categories to set limits

6. Tick the box next to a category to limit it. You can choose from different categories like Social Networking, Creative, Entertainment and others

7. If you would like to see the different apps that will be limited, hit the expand icon.

8. You can set the limit in the **Time** section after you have selected the app category. Depending on your preference, you can choose to use a Custom schedule or just to set it for Every Day.

9. Do the same steps for the other categories you want to limit and hit **Done** when you are through.

If you would like to remove the limits for an app

- Enter the **Screen Time** settings and choose the account you want to remove the limit for

- In the panel along the left side of the screen, select **App Limits**

Find the app category you don't want to limit anymore and untick the box.

Find My computer

Find My, according to Apple, helps to track lost devices. Data will be sent from different devices until you get the data you need to track it. This way, you still have hope of getting your Mac even after you lose it

1. Summon Spotlight by pressing **Cmd + Space** and enter **Find My** in the field
2. Select **Device** in the upper left corner
3. Choose the name of the device you would like to track
- This will then present it to you on the map. To see other options, hit the **i** icon. You could also get directions to the location

Modify the sidebar in Finder

If you didn't know yet, Finder serves as a file browser on your device. One awesome thing about it is that it can be customized to suit your royal taste very easily.

If there's a folder that you regularly open, you can save time by clipping to the sidebar in Finder.

Move to the folder you want to add to the sidebar

Drag the folder to the sidebar

If you would like to add apps, press and hold **Cmd** and move the icons to the sidebar

Edit folder icons

One thing you'll be used to as a user of a Mac is the beautiful aesthetic. One major selling point for MacBooks from the start is the amazing interface that Apple provides in their systems. But another thing Apple is known for is not providing many customization options.

Fortunately, if the folder icons don't suit your style, you can replace it easily with icons that you think would fit best. Another reason people do this is so that they can easily identify which folder is which without having to hover on it. By adding your own images you can tell the different folders apart

And it isn't really that hard to do this, you don't even need to install some third-party app. If you would like to customize the thumbnail images that show up for your folders,

1. Find the photo you would like to use as the icon and double click it so that it will come up in the Preview app on your computer

2. Get to the Select All option by pressing **Cmd + A** or you can click **Edit** in the menu bar and choose **Select All** from the dropdown

3. Get to the Copy option by pressing **Cmd + C** or you can click **Edit** in the menu bar and choose **Copy** from the dropdown

4. Move to the folder that you want to change the icon of and right click on it. From the menu that shows up, click on **Get Info**

5. Select the icon for the folder in the upper left of the Info window.

6. Paste the image by pressing **Cmd + V** or you can click **Edit** and choose **Paste** from the dropdown

You can change back to the default icon if you change your mind in the future. When you select **Get Info**, choose the folder icon and hit **Cmd + X** to cut the image out. You can also select **Edit** in the menu bar and click **Cut**.

Crop images in Preview

One app that doesn't get enough attention is Preview on the Mac. It's very capable and it makes a lot of these tricks possible. There are times when you need to perform a simple task without enlisting the help of Photoshop (which is very expensive by the way). Times like this call for Preview

Simply open up the image you want to use in Preview and go through the menu and dozens of options the app gives you. One of the things you can do is to crop an image. It's like a simple thing but not many apps allow you to do this.

Rather than open some expensive photo editing app, just use the Rectangular Selection tool in Preview to draw a selection on the parts of the photo you want to keep and pick Crop from the different tools. You can also press **Cmd + K** to use it faster.

If you don't want to make a standard rectangle selection, you can also select Smart Lasso or Instant Alpha tool to draw more complicated selections in Preview

Get the Wi-Fi password for your devices

To help you deal with passwords, your Mac has a feature called Keychain. This gives the Mac the ability to recall the passwords you've used before so you can use them in the future if necessary. Keychain Access is the program that comes with Keychain and it is here your secret information is kept.

You might think you wouldn't use this much but when it comes to Wi-Fi connections, it does come in handy. Like for example, if for some reason, you don't remember your Wi-Fi password, the Keychain feature can help you find it.

1. Simply launch **Keychain Access**. You can get to the software quickly by using Spotlight to search for it
2. Look for the connection. Double click the Keychain that matches the SSID you need
3. Choose the option for **Show Password** and add your general Keychain password to gain access.

4. If you entered it correctly, you will be able to see
    the password that you need.

Set your own keyboards shortcuts

Even if you are not a fan of keyboard shortcuts, you should know that they are beneficial for one thing and one thing only; to save time. Nobody wants to spend the time to click **Menu**, **General**, then **Edit** to get to a feature when you can press 2 keys on the keyboard and save 5 seconds.

If you find that you use a menu option so many times and you can't find a shortcut for it, simply make one yourself. To do this on your computer

1. Fire the System Preferences menu by clicking the Apple menu at the top left corner of the screen then choose **System Preferences**
2. Select **Keyboard**
3. Then **App Shortcuts**
4. Hit the plus **+** button to create a shortcut
5. From the dropdown list, select the apps you want the shortcut to apply to. You want to make sure

that you know the name of the command to be entered in the following field.

6. Pick the key combination that will summon the command. Finalize the selection by selecting **Add**

Grouping notifications in the Notification Center

Back in the day, items were grouped in the Notification Center according to their apps. The method is different now and items are now grouped by their respective dates. This means that all the notifications that you receive today will appear grouped together.

This is helpful so that you don't have to look through the notifications you decided to ignore the previous day. But if you are not a fan of this new method but would like to revert back to the former system, you can do so in the System Preferences menu

1. Click the Apple menu at the top left corner of the screen and choose **System Preferences**
2. Select **Notifications**
3. You can adjust the sort order to suit your taste in the Notification Center Sort Order menu

Remotely view someone else's screen

If you are trying to help someone fix a problem on their Mac, one very simple method to view their screen and to even control their system via the internet is to use Screen Sharing. You can easily search for it with Spotlight after which you will have to add the Apple ID of the friend you want to help.

Simply ask them for the Apple ID and they should tell you if they need your help. If they don't know their Apple ID for some reason, tell them to enter System Preferences and they'll find it in the iCloud panel. While they're in the System Preferences, you also want them to turn on Screen Sharing in the Sharing section.

To block intruders, they'll have to grant you access to view their screen. To grant you the permission to view their screen, they can just hit Screen Sharing located in the menu bar. Once they've allowed access, you will be able to not only view their screen, but also control their keyboard

and mouse easily

Send iMessages on your Mac

Applications on iOS and iPadOS have slowly made their way to the macOS and this includes apps like Apple Books, Maps, Notes and of course Messages. On your Mac, you have the Message app and this allows you to send iMessages and also SMS messages. The best part about this is that you don't need your iPhone to be present

On your Mac, there are 2 kinds of messages that you can receive and send. With the help of the servers from Apple, you are able to send messages with iMessages. But when it comes to regular text messages, they go through your iPhone

If you would like to send a text on your MacBook
In the dock, select the **Messages** icon. (if you don't know it, it the blue icon with a speech bubble). You can also search for it with Spotlight
You'll want to make sure that you log in with the Apple ID that is connected to your iOS device

Just next to the search box, hit the icon to create a new message

In the **To** section, enter the email address or number of the person you would like to contact. If you are using the email address, make sure that the email address is connected to their iMessage.

You can also hit the plus **+** icon to add friends from your contact if your contacts are synced with your computer

The contact you are trying to reach will have a blue box if they have an iPhone. What this means is that your text will be gotten via iMessage. Depending on how your contact info is registered on their device, you may be identified as the sender via your email address and not necessarily your number.

Simply type in your message in the iMessage field if the contact has iMessage

Use a different screenshot file type

You probably take multiple screenshots in a day. It's a super easy way to capture a funny meme you find on the internet so that you can share it with your friends later. When you take a screenshot on your Mac, it will be saved as a PNG file.

This could be a good thing because PNG files tend to carry more information but it could also be a burden because the file size can also be larger than jpegs.

If you would like your screenshots to be saved as the regular jpeg image, enter the Terminal on your computer. You'll want to enter exactly this; ***defaults write com.apple.screencapture type JPG***. After you type that, press **Enter**.

Once you restart your computer, the change will kick in and all screenshots will be saved as jpegs. You can force it to happen right away if you don't want to do a restart, simply enter this; ***KillAll SystemUIServer***. When you type that in, press **Enter**. If you want to go back to the default PNG format, type this instead; ***defaults write com.apple.screencapture type PNG.***

How to share purchases with family members

You are able to share your purchases with 6 people via the family sharing function in macOS. This could sound attractive to you as a parent because it would grant you the power to reject purchases made with your card by your children on the App Store.

Then there are other perks like being able to pinpoint their location and have a joint calendar. Setting this up couldn't be easier especially with the new macOS Catalina

1. Enter the **System Preferences** section
2. Just next to the option for Apple ID, select **Family Sharing**.

How to record your screen on the Mac

If you would like to record your screen on macOS Catalina

1. Hit the **Shift + Cmd + 5** combo on the keyboard and this will fire up the Screenshot feature

2. At the bottom of the screen, you'll see a control bar. If you are interested in getting a still image of the screen, use this to take a screenshot right away. But you'll need to do more if you want to record the screen

3. Select **Options** in the control bar to tweak the settings. Like for example, you are able to enable the microphone, specify the location the recording should be saved to and also set a timer.

4. If you would like to record just a section of the screen, hit the button just beside Options with a dotted line outline and a dot at the edge corner. If you would like to record the entire screen hit the button with a firm outline and a dot at the edge

5. When you select the portion of the screen you want to record, hit the **Record** button next to Options. Click any area on the screen to record if you choose to record the entire screen

6. When you are done recording, you can stop it by hitting the stop button in the top corner of the menu bar. If you are a fan of shortcuts, **Cmd + Ctrl + Esc** will end it quickly

3

MacOS Catalina Music

Navigating the Music app

iTunes has been replaced by the Music app on macOS Catalina. This now provides a new way to play music on your computer. But this doesn't mean that when you install Catalina on your MacBook, your songs will simply vanish into thin air. No, you don't have to worry, your music collection will simply be transported into the Music app.

This means that you don't have to transfer anything when you get the new macOS. The only thing that can be considered a problem is that you'll need to get to know the new Music app because it isn't quite the same as iTunes.

The name 'Music app', shouldn't be new to you if you've used an iPod, iPad or an iPhone over the years. The app has been available on iOS but it only just came to the Mac with macOS Catalina. With the same app on both your tablet, smartphone and your computer, music can be synced across your different Apple devices.

If your music library is full of tracks, it could get cumbersome and a bit chaotic. One of the things you'll want to learn how to do on the Music app is finding the right tracks easily

Finding a track on the Music app

If you would like to play a certain song or album, you can get to it through different means.

There's a navigational menu on the left side of the Music app. From this section, you'll find different categories connected to Apple Music like Browse, For You and Radio. If you are subscribed to Apple, you can explore that section.

But this isn't where you'll find your personal music collection. Just below the Apple Music section is your Library where you'll get the different Albums, Artist, Songs and Recently Added categories. Any song in your collection will be found here.

The track should be on Mac and you listen to it right away. But this is not always the case, it will be different if you use the iCloud Music Library. With this, your songs will be kept in iCloud and when you select a track to play, it will have to be streamed. You can download it on your computer when you hit the cloud symbol.

With the **Recently Added** section, you can find any new content. This includes items that you've gotten from Apple Music, iTunes or transferred to your computer with another method. The other section; **Songs**, **Artists** and **Albums** group tracks according to their names. So if you click **Albums**, it opens up your Albums library.

With the Albums section, you'll find the artwork for the albums displayed on the page. It doesn't do anything for your songs, really, but the collection simply looks pleasing and visually appealing if you have downloaded the artwork for the Album

Just under the section for Library is **Playlist**. Your playlists will be featured here.

If you would like to play music on your computer, you simply just look for the song in your library and click on it. After the track you chose has ended, the track that plays next will vary depending on how you have things set up.

To play music from an album, you need to look for the song in the Album section. After the song finishes, the other songs in the album will be played as well. If you don't want the songs to play in a particular order, simply hit the Shuffle icon (it depicts 2 arrows crossing).

This also works if you would like to play different songs sung by the same artist. Simply look for the song in the Artist section.

Even if you have enabled Shuffle, you could also find out the songs that will be played next.

Select the **3-line icon** at the top right hand corner of the page

Choose the **Up Next** option. This presents the songs that will be played next on the Playlist

When you hover on any of the songs, you'll see the icon that allows you to remove the track from the list.

Repeating a track

If you choose a song and you really like what you hear, you can decide to listen to it on repeat. Unlike the straightforward way to do it in iTunes, the process of repeating a track with the Music app is different.

1. To repeat the track
2. Hit **Controls** from the menu
3. Select **Repeat**
4. Tap on the option for **One** to play this one song on repeat.

Skip a song

One thing that will likely happen, especially when you are listening to songs on repeat, is encountering songs that you don't really like or not in the mood to listen to. If you would like to skip the song, simply select the icon for fast forward. You'll find the icon just next to the play button.

One awesome thing you can do in the Music app is to make a playlist only for the tracks that you've skipped. If you really don't like these songs, grouping them in one playlist allows you to get rid of them once and for all.

Delete a song

Speaking of getting rid of songs, it's really easy to remove a song from your library

1. Find the track you would like to get rid of and right click on it

2. From the menu that shows up, select **Delete From Library**

3. You would get a notification asking if you also want to remove the song from the iCloud Music Library (you'll only get this if you've got iTunes match)

4. Choose the option for **Delete Song**

Using the TV app on your Mac

Just when you think It couldn't get any better, macOS Catalina makes another feature possible for the Mac. Provided by Apple, Apple TV is the main hub to get all your TV shows and movies. The TV app on iOS made it possible for users of the iPhone to watch their favorite titles.

But with macOS Catalina, you also get the TV app on your Mac. One top feature of the app is syncing. The progress made in your movies is tracked and synced across your Apple devices so that you can start watching where you left off on another device.

This doesn't mean that there aren't differences between the TV app on the iPhone and that on the Mac, after all, they run on different operating systems. One main difference is that there are certain apps that can work with TV app on your iPhone but you don't get on the Mac.

For example, the TV app on iPhone works nicely with services like NBC and Hulu so that you can get your favorite movies and TV shows easily. But since you don't get these kinds of apps on the macOS, you won't be able to use them with the Mac's version of the TV app

If you would like to watch a show on the TV app for the Mac, this is how you'll do it

1. From the **Applications** folder or the Dock, launch the **TV app**

2. You can choose from the different sections to watch a movie or TV show. You can select **What To Watch**, **Up Next** or any other available category

3. When you find something you want to watch, click on it

4. Select the **Play** button

Adding shows to the Up Next Category

1. If you are looking for a TV show or movie to watch, one section you'll want to look into is the **Up Next** section. From here, you'll easily find the latest episodes of some of your most desired TV shows. If you would like to add content to this category,
2. Launch the **TV app**
3. Look for the TV show or movie you would like to send to the Up Next section.
4. When you play a TV show or movie, it will be sent to the Up Next section automatically
5. Another way to add content to Up Next is to select it from the other categories and select **Add To Up Next**

How to buy TV shows or movies

1. If you are tired of watching the content you have already purchased, you can get more from the TV app. To buy TV shows and movies from the TV app
2. Launch the **TV app** on the Mac
3. Along the top of the screen, choose **TV Shows** or **Movies**
4. Look for the title you would like to purchase and select it
5. Hit the **Buy** button. You can also rent content by selecting the **Rent** button.

If you know the exact movie or TV show you want to purchase,

- Click the search bar at the top of the screen
- Type in the title of the movie or TV show
- Select the title when it comes up in the search results
- Select the **Buy** button

How to subscribe to channels

You can also subscribe to channels with the TV app on your Mac.

1. Fire up the **TV app**
2. Look for a channel you would like to subscribe to
3. Select **Try It For Free**
4. When prompted to add your password, comply
5. Hit **Buy** and then **Confirm**

Using Airplay

If you are looking to share content from your Apple device to a Smart TV, there's no better way than to use Airplay. With this, sharing photos, videos and music is a breeze. It's also ideal for those who want to mirror their Mac to a larger TV display.

To use Airplay on your Mac

1. You'll want your Smart TV and computer to be on the same Wi-Fi network.

2. Look for the video that you would like to play via Airplay. You can do this with Safari

3. Hit the Apple icon at the upper left corner of the screen and choose **System Preferences**

4. Among the myriads of options, select **Displays**

5. Along the bottom of the display, turn on Airplay if it's disabled. It's not enough to turn on Airplay, you also want to tick the box for **Show mirroring options in the menu bar when available**.

6. In the menu bar at the top of the screen, you'll find the Airplay icon. If you don't know it, it's the icon that depicts a monitor.

7. From the dropdown menu that appears, choose your Smart TV. This is also the same process you'll follow if you would like to disable Airplay. Simply choose **Turn Off AirPlay**.

If your smart TV is compatible, you can also mirror the screen of your computer to the TV.

For this to work, you'll want your Smart TV and computer to be on the same Wi-Fi network.

Select the Airplay icon along the menu bar at the very top of the screen.

Select the compatible TV you would like to mirror your computer to

You'll find a passcode on your TV screen. Copy this passcode on your computer

If you would like to disable screen mirroring, you'll have to disable Airplay.

Create a music playlist

Playlists allow you to group your favorite songs in one place. You can create playlists on the Music app for the Mac but there are 2 main methods to do this.

The common method is to manually create a playlist and add music to the playlist yourself. The other method is to use the Smart Playlist feature. With this, songs are added to a particular playlist according to the rules you set.

To create a playlist

1. Select **File** then **New**

2. Choose **New Playlist** and add a name to the playlist. The playlist will now show up on the sidebar of the Music app

To add songs to the playlist, find the song in any of the categories in the sidebar of the app. You can also easily search for the song.

Drag the song to the playlist in the sidebar.

To create smart playlists on your Mac

- Enter the **Music app** and select **File**. Choose **New**

- Click on **Smart Playlist**

- Add the rules for including songs to a playlist

4

Browsing the Web and Emailing

Browse the web with Safari

As part of the macOS, you get the Safari web browser app on your MacBook. If you're not a fan of the browser, you are not stuck with it. Apple still allows you to install other browsers like Chrome or Dolphin Browser and use those for your web browsing desires.

For the average user, Safari should do well and it really doesn't lack much of the top features that third-party apps provide. If you just got a MacBook, you would need some assistance in finding your way around the browser. Even old-time Safari folks could also grab a trick or two from this section.

Before you start exploring all that Safari has to offer, you want to ensure that your version of Safari is the latest. If you would like to find out the Safari version you have,

1. Enter the **Safari** app
2. Select **Safari** then choose **About Safari**

3.   This shows you the version of the app you've got

But since the app comes built into the operating system, basically, your Safari browser should be up to date if you are running the latest macOS version. Even though you can still get the latest version of Safari while running an older macOS version, it'll be better to update to the latest one so that you get other new features

How to browse with Safari

At the top of the window in Safari is the big bar that allows you to search for terms and get to different web pages or to add the URL of a website. By default, the search engine will be set to Google but if you want to use some other like Bing, you have the freedom to change it.

If you have visited a site before, you don't really have to enter the complete URL to get to the website. Simply type in a couple letters of the URL and the rest will be auto-filled for you. If you've entered **twitter.com** before. Simply type in ***twit*** and the rest of the letters will be completed for you. You just have to hit enter and you'll be taken to the site.

Find favorites in Safari

If you would like to get to websites you visit frequently, Safari presents you with different options. Opening a new tab will allow you to see the sites you frequently visit as well as the ones in your Favorites view. You can tweak things so that the Tops Sites view can be shown.

1. Enter **Safari**

2. Select **Preferences**

3. Choose **General**

4. Just beside **New tabs open with**, select the menu

From here you can set new tabs to open showing an Empty Page, the Same Page, Top Sites or the Homepage. If you select the Top Sites option, you can choose to show as few as 6 sites or as much as 24. To get rid of or add Top Sites, move the cursor over on the preview and it will show you the Pin icon as well as the **X** icon

Select the **X** icon for the sites that you don't want to see again and hit the Pin icon for the ones you would like to store. Most of the time, the Top Sites view shows the sites that you visit regularly.

Another awesome thing that will really save time is to pin a site to the menu bar. If you know that you binge-watch YouTube videos regularly or you look through Instagram on your computer, you can pin the shortcut to the menu bar for swift and easy access.

If you would like to pin a site,

Enter the URL of the site in the address bar and hit Enter

Right click on the tab the site was loaded. You can also control click.

Select **Pin Tab**

Access websites quickly with bookmarks

One common way of keeping your favorite web pages is bookmarking them. If you would like to quickly access certain sites, bookmarking them allows you to go back to them later without entering the URL over again

1. To add a site to your bookmarks
2. Fire up the **Safari** app from Finder or the Dock at the bottom of the screen
3. Enter the website URL in the address bar
4. One quick way of adding the site to your bookmarks is to use Keyboard shortcuts. On your keyboard hit the **Cmd + D** combo

5. Add the bookmark title and description. These fields are not necessary so you can skip it if you want.

6. Select **Add**

If you've added sites you regularly visit to your bookmarks, then you need a way to view your bookmarks quickly. To see all your bookmarks,

- ➤ Fire up the **Safari** app from Finder or the Dock at the bottom of the screen
- ➤ Next to the address bar in the Safari app, hit the show sidebar button
- ➤ If you don't find it there already, it the **Bookmarks tab**

As you add new pages to your bookmarks, there'll be older ones you'll want to remove. It could be because you don't use them anymore or the site has been taken down. To remove a webpage from your bookmarks

- ➤ Fire up the **Safari** app from Finder or the Dock at the bottom of the screen
- ➤ In the menu bar at the upper left side of the screen, select **Bookmarks**

- ➢ Choose the option for **Edit Bookmarks**

- ➢ Just beside **Favorites**, select the arrow

- ➢ Look for the bookmark you would like to delete and right click on it. You can also control click on the bookmark to be removed

- ➢ Select **Delete**

Keep a reading list of web pages

When you add web pages to your reading list, you are able to go back to the page and read it at a later date. What makes reading lists cool is the fact that you can view them even when you don't have an internet connection

1. Fire up the **Safari** app from Finder or the Dock at the bottom of the screen
2. In the address bar on the screen, enter the URL of the website you want to include in the reading list
3. On your keyboard, hit the **Cmd + Shift + D** combo

Since you have saved web pages to your reading list, you should know how to actually view the reading list so that you can view the sites that have been saved

1. Fire up the **Safari** app from Finder or the Dock at the bottom of the screen

2. Just beside the address bar, select the show sidebar button

3. Select the tab for **Reading List**. If you don't know this, it basically depicts reading glasses

4. Find the page you would like to open and click it

5. If you are done going through the page on the reading list, you can delete it so that useless pages don't clutter the entire section

6. Fire up the **Safari** app from Finder or the Dock at the bottom of the screen

7. Just beside the address bar, select the show sidebar button

8. Select the tab for **Reading List**

9. Right click on the webpage you would like to get rid of

10. Choose **Remove Item**

Navigate among open web pages using tabs

Safari allows you to open several tabs in one window. So instead of opening multiple Safari windows just to enter a site, you can have numerous pages in just that one window. The benefit of opening tabs is that it provides quick access to the web pages and it makes browsing less chaotic.

Opening a new tab in Safari is easy, simply hit the **Cmd + T** combo on the keyboard.

To the right of the address bar, you'll find an icon showing 2 squares. When you select this, you see all the web pages on the window in thumbnail view. On the tabs that you've opened, you will also find the name of the webpage.

If you've opened one too many tabs in a Safari window, you'll have to close it to declutter. To do this, simply move your mouse to the tab and you'll see the **X** button appear around the corner of the tab. Click on it to get rid of the tab

If you want to close all of the tabs except for one, press and hold **Option + Alt** as you press the **X** button to close the rest of the other open tabs.

Tighten up Safari's security

While Apple updates Safari to make browsing faster and much more comfortable, another area Apple is always looking to improve on is security.

There are many fraudulent websites around but Safari has a brilliant way of identifying them. The browser can recognize a site that uses encryption and one that does not. With the help of Google Safe Browsing tech, Safari can also warn you if you are entering a scammy site or one with malware

> Select **Preferences** from the Safari menu
> Along the top of the window, enter the **Security** tab
> Turn on the option for **Warn when visiting a fraudulent website**

With this feature turned on, the browser will present a full-screen warning if you ever enter any of these malicious sites.

If you don't want advertisers to keep track of your browsing behavior and present you with relevant ads, then you can try preventing Cross Site Tracking

> ➤ Select **Preferences** from the Safari menu

> ➤ Along the top of the window, enter the **Security** tab

> ➤ Find the option for **Prevent Cross Site Tracking** and tick the box. Just below that, also tick the box for **Ask websites not to track me**

Do keep in mind that this doesn't always work. After all, you are still 'asking' the site not to you track you. Really, then, if the website decides not to honor the appeal there's nothing you can do about it.

If you would like to clear your browsing history from Safari,

> ➤ Select **Clear History** from the Safari menu

> ➤ Select how much history you would like to clear

> ➤ Choose the option for **Clear history**

➤ When you select Clear history, your browsing history will also be cleared from other devices if you have enabled Safari in iCloud

Manage your app and website passwords

If you're looking to manage your app or website passwords on your Mac, It doesn't get better than iCloud keychain.

1. From the top left corner of the menu bar, hit the Apple logo. Select the option for **System Preferences**
2. Select **iCloud**
3. Tick the checkbox for **Keychain**
4. Input the password for your Apple ID
5. Select **OK**

To be able to set up iCloud keychain on a different device, add a 6 – digit code. You'll have to confirm the code after you've entered it

Add your mobile number. Make sure that you are able to receive SMS messages on that number

If you would like to view all your passwords on iCloud keychain,

> ➢ Fire up the Safari app
> ➢ Along the upper left corner of the screen, select **Safari**
> ➢ Choose **Preferences**, then **Passwords**
> ➢ Enter the password for your Mac, keep in mind that this is not the same as the password for your Apple ID
> ➢ Select the site you would like to view the password for

Reply to or forward an email message

1. Open up the **Mail** app on your computer and select the message you want to reply to or forward
2. From the header of your message, choose any of the actions you would like to take. This includes **Reply** and **Forward**
3. Enter the text you want to reply with.
4. Some messages could have attachments and if the original message you are replying to has one, you can choose to skip or include them
5. Hit the **Send** button when you are done.

Disclaimers

In as much as the author believes beginners will find this book helpful in learning how to use the MacOS Catalina device, it is only a small book. It should not be relied upon solely for all MacOS Catalina tricks and troubleshooting.

About the Author

Ryan is a first class marketing strategist and tech enthusiast who has written several wireless industry trade articles.